THE COLOR OF REBIRTH

Memoirs of Faith, Land, and Renewal

By

Luz Diaz

ISBN: 978-1-970435-56-6

Published By: Ink Founders

Dedication

~ 3 ~

To my mother Paula,

whose hands never let me go—

not on the muddy roads, not in the storms.

To my children, Celeddy and Álvaro,

who are living proof that miracles exist.

To my grandmother,

whose stories wove the fabric of my soul,

and to the Virgin of Altagracia,

who always granted me peace.

"I fell, I rose, and I kept going. That was my journey."

— Luz Diaz

Table of Contents

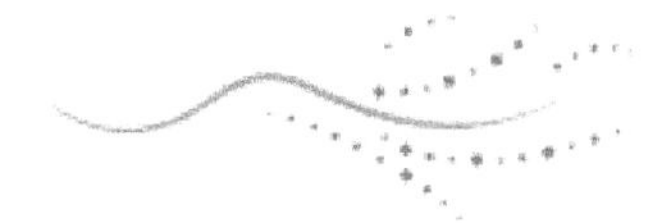

Preface

This book was born on the margins of life: on a dirt road, in a field where the wind smelled of grass and promise, in the early hours of childbirth without a doctor, and in nights of prayer without a roof. It is the story of a woman the world did not expect to survive, and who not only survived, but found in every breaking point a seed of color.

The pages that follow have not been touched by the hand of fiction. They are memories, with all their roughness and truth. The voice that narrates them is the same one that prayed before the Virgin of Altagracia in her darkest hours; the same one that sang to her newborn children in conditions that defy imagination, the same one that today, with a heart at peace, chooses to share her journey with the world.

To read these pages is to walk through the Dominican countryside barefoot, to feel the warmth of the cooking fire, to hear the sound of the river, and to understand that faith is not an abstract concept: it is a white horse that carries you back home even when you do not know where home is.

May this book remind whoever reads it that pain does not define destiny; that miracles sometimes arrive in American trucks; and that there is always, always, a new color waiting on the other side of rebirth.

— Luz Diaz

Author's Note

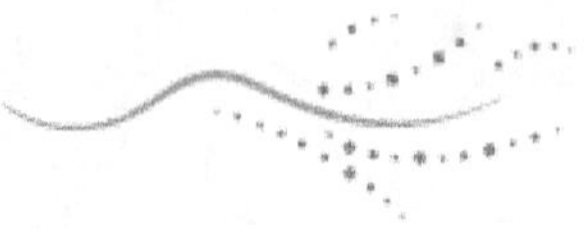

The names of some individuals mentioned in these memoirs have been preserved exactly as I remember them; others have been omitted to protect their privacy. The places, dates, and events reflect my memory as I hold it, with the clarity that love provides, and the opacity that pain sometimes imposes.

This is not a book about perfection. It is a book about trying. About getting back up. About continuing.

If you recognize yourself in these pages, in the exhaustion or in the joy, it is because this story is yours as well.

Chapter I

The First Colors

Childhood in the Fields

*"The days passed, full of beautiful memories, because I
was born to love, to live, and to remember."*

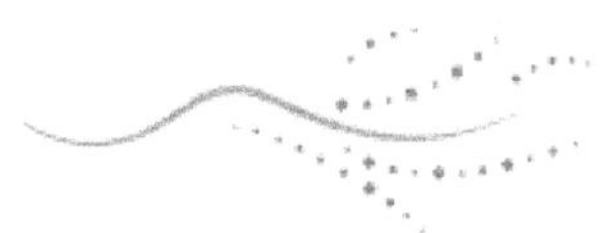

I was born on July 7, 1980, at four o'clock on a Friday morning. My mother, Paula, was born on March 5, 1945, on my grandfather Antonio's farm. My father, his goats, and I were deeply happy, even though those years often felt uncertain.

As a child, I was immensely happy riding horses. My horse was white, and it always carried me to cut grass for my goats. At 5:30 in the morning, with the sack already in my hand, I would gather grass to feed my animals. My thoughts belonged only to the wind, the scent of the grass, and how the breeze filled me with strength.

A house made of palm leaves, wooden planks, and earthen floors—that was the life of a young shepherd in the countryside. The days passed full of beautiful memories, because I was born to know how to love, to live, and to remember.

My grandfather passed away in 1990, and soon after, my grandmother died on April 4th. It was painful to leave behind the land where I grew up, but it was no longer my home. As I grew, I ventured farther away. Years later, I had an old chestnut (reddish) horse, one with a clear gaze and a spirit as vast as the fields.

I'd walk through Chaparral and the sandy fields, happy. But then, when my father told me I could no longer go so far, I went on as if with my eyes closed. I counted the wind, my memories, and the countryside. When I felt pain, the memory was so strong it pierced me. But time, as they say, heals everything.

Climbing the stairs of the past, I climbed toward the sky and my faith in the Lord Jesus. I always walked with that faith, for people so often stop believing. And so, to the very end, with faith as my guide, I walked through the countryside; I fell, I rose, and I kept going. That was my journey.

Chapter II

The Cold of December

December 17, 1995

"With pain—but always walking."

An idea took root in my heart, a great idea for a song. I was only fifteen years old. I wished my father would come looking for me, that he would find me. My heart told me it was cold and raining; a cruel December. It was December of 1995, and I was freezing, shivering at everything around me.

Eating little, my mother would say, "Everything is in your neck." When I feel a lump in that part of my body, I tell myself it is nothing, but I can always feel the pain. Then my thoughts return to the wind, to the horse, and to my memories. This is my life: with pain, but always moving forward.

On a road I could no longer endure, I lay down, and my mother reached out her hand to me. I never forgot that. She brought me a poncho, coats, socks, and even shoes for my size 40 feet. But nothing healed me. My mother gave me tea, and my stomach settled, but a deep pain rose on both sides of my body; a pain that would not stop.

I did not know why. The bathrooms, the presence of others, even companionship felt like a coffin, far from home. No one bought me a Coca-Cola but myself. She gave me underwear and other essentials, the things a body needs.

Moments like these are difficult to recall. When I sit now, I cannot bear the pain; I still feel it. Even the simple act of going to the bathroom was torment; I would fall from the bed trying. I tried to push away that immense pain by remembering happier times, but it was useless. I would leave the house to eat, and the need to use the bathroom would return. I would go back, sit down, and still feel the urge, but the pain remained. Then, while in the bathroom, tormented by pain, I felt a lump at the front of my ribcage. But I carried on.

It was then that beautiful thoughts of faith came to me, and finally, a positive idea arrived. When I think about that lump and the pain that does not go away, I know what is happening in my mind. I feel a little of that, opa, it stays just there, the pain and the same restricted movement in my foot. It put me in a state almost like a coma. That was how I came out of the bathroom and lay down.

Like my mother, when the pains come one after another, they do not move. I think about everything: my schoolwork, my feet, the part of me that no longer rises. My mother's support was my backbone. I held my chest with one hand and grasped the child's fingers with the other. I pulled and pushed, telling them everything. They told me, "Pull here; the pain will go away." I felt as if I had a doll or something; I truly did not know. I only asked heaven to help me so that the child's pain would go away.

When my mother saw me holding my back, already without strength, I was just a child, a child sobbing. I moved with every ounce of strength I had. I was as if dead; I did not cry. And then, it happened.

It bent slightly at the end, like a poncho. For the hat, I used a piece of that same half-poncho. I did not know what to do; I was so desperate. We could not go to the doctor because the ground was soaked. We lost so much. Everything was bitter.

Chapter III

The Miracle of Life

When God Answered

"From this day forward, I am, I am not. I know that God exists."

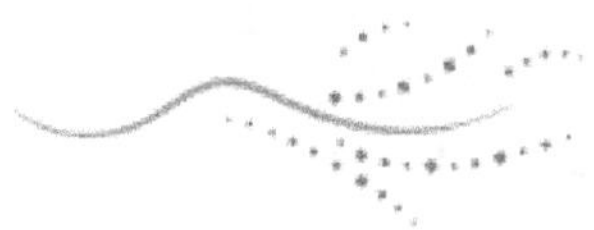

Then, a beautiful American truck arrived. In my pain, I lay thinking of home and of light. We were so desperate to remove the mass that had adhered to the placenta, trapped inside me. I thought it was because I had not moved enough. But when the baby was born, my father believed everything had already come out. He was floating in it, and she told him, "Father, the weight… it is because they have it. It is heavy." They placed a bottle of warm water on my abdomen, and finally, I expelled it.

That was a miracle. What I had asked for came to pass just fifteen minutes after the birth. I said: "From this day forward, I am, I am not. I know that God exists."

Three days later, I was able to see a doctor to be examined, and so was the child. To my amazement, it was a miracle. The pediatricians said that my son had taken the same step I had taken with God, because the child was perfect.

It was as if I had not gone through labor at all, especially given my condition. I had been very thin, and I had always hated the pain of pregnancy. No one truly knew the pain I was in, but I knew that child was mine. My belly had never grown much; it never swelled during those months. That was something magnificent, inexplicable to anyone who has not lived it. That is how I came to write about my experience.

As time passed, my son grew up healthy, just as the doctor had predicted. He never suffered an infection. I worked collecting coconuts, and the child stayed by my side. It was a good life; we lacked nothing, and we were very happy.

When my father got down from the truck, he would say "contract" while cleaning the farm. My brother and I lived there, working alongside him. We did not mind the work; it was simply what we did. We had a well for water, and in the afternoons, we helped our father with tasks like mending our clothes.

Christmas was a time of great celebration. My son received new clothes and a suitcase, all paid for with the earnings from the farm. Mr. and Mrs. Rojas Quiribo were humble and kind, showing our family great love. Later, I moved to a dry farm where my parents worked and tried to work there as well. My brother had been born on a cocoa farm, a place of plants and soil full of blessings.

As time went on and my son grew, I moved again, this time in with my siblings. In time, I took charge of another farm where I raised chickens and pigs and planted coconuts. And so the cycle continued.

My second child was born, and I had the same miraculous experience with him as with my first; God guided me through it. I never strayed far from the house or the cooking fire. I walked among coconut palms and banana trees until I reached the place my father had found for us, near a beautiful river. The house was well kept and not far from town, about an hour's walk. My father, my mother, and my child were all with me.

This time, the difference was that I cut the umbilical cord of my first child with wet scissors, and I did the same with the second. But once again, I had a problem with the placenta. My father, in a hurry, sent someone for help. They went to a polyclinic, a rural hospital where a very kind and humble doctor worked.

I arrived around 6:00 AM in that same difficult condition. Thanks to God, they took me to the city of San Francisco. I remember the pain, but the doctor attended to me herself, and everything turned out well. I was discharged on December 16, 1997. Later, I moved again.

I went to live in a small wooden house in a more populated countryside, and eventually, my father's side of the family also lived there. My children were growing. For me, any place is good: the countryside, the town, anywhere. I have never liked going around visiting; my mother used to say many things about that. What sustained me was the light, the fire, the passing years, and destiny.

Little by little, our area became more like a town. But we were poor, and by then I already had my second daughter. My mother stayed with the eldest son. For me, it felt like a deserted corner of the world. In the distance, the city of San Francisco could be seen. They said a cyclone had swept through the city, carrying away the poverty and the bicycles. I had never seen a cyclone.

I remained the same, but I felt as though my soul had abandoned me. The warmth of God felt heavy amidst so much poverty. As a person of peace, I clung to my faith. There was a small church built on stilts where God stayed with my little girl. In the end, I found myself in the street. Everything was gone, save for a few old plastic chairs.

The Virgin of Altagracia

Faith in Desolation

"Because God does not fail."

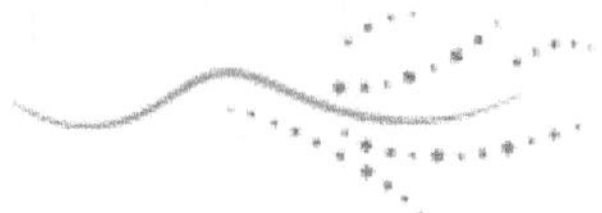

God help me, Virgin of Altagracia. Do not leave me alone, I beg of you. As I had nowhere to live, I had to go to the Church of the Virgin of Altagracia, where many displaced people were staying on each floor. Humbly, I did not feel it in my spirit, because God does not fail. There was a neighbor of mine, God rest her soul, Mrs. Rosa, the wife of Mr. Calo. What a person she was. May God hold her in His glory and grant her abundant peace and health.

The children were small. Medina's faith was within me. As a young woman, like many others, I was treated like family. There was always someone who shared their food with me, so I would not have to face loneliness.

After some time, the president helped all the displaced people. With faith, I was given the light of my mother. I thank God. Finally, I was able to have my milk. My parents went to Santiago. Time passed. He could not make up his mind. I went to try my luck in Santiago, where my father took me and my children.

With time, I began working to build a small business and support my son. I would never leave my son behind. My father had a little house in that neighborhood. Time passed, and my son moved forward. I also worked, caring for children. I had a good companion, but later I had another who was not so good; a promoter of neediness.

I was always raising goats, but the world of work was something entirely different. I remember my grandfather above all for his humility. Thank God. Here, everything is beautiful. People ride horses, which is wonderful.

Climbing a hill was just as beautiful, where people would go to collect coconuts, cut them down, and sell them. We ate the coconuts and drank the water; how beautiful nature is. Thank God, in every region, the trees of the countryside are never lacking.

I was always the happiest girl in the world during my childhood. I remember climbing onto the dough cart and riding around. I grew up on the coast, playing on the ground, barefoot on a mattress of banana leaves. We played, and my grandmother gave us more leaves to play with. What a beautiful life.

Thanks to my father, I remember my father, my brother, and my family. We did not work only for ourselves; it was always for our children. Many years have passed since I was with my mother's family. They were humble, good people. Thank you, Father God. This is who I am.

In the past, we would look for hills to gather things to sell, all while living in that blind property. When the sun rose, we had mattresses to sell, and that was support, our entire economy. It was very difficult, but it was an unforgettable, beautiful, and very happy time.

That is why nothing remains now; the events do not erase themselves. But this mouth is so beautiful. It's natural for me to say: this world is for all time. That is life, and it is beautiful.

I thank God for my family and for all the things in life. For marrying, for my grandfather, Rafael, and my grandmother, who was so beloved. For the beautiful memories, for the countryside, and for the sky. Fortunately, there was the family of Titonci, and I always loved them.

Then my father decided to move to other places. With the passage of time, we were entering the area near Benito. I received my move. It was the ranch, the road, Aguacatillo. That ranch was beautiful, full of coconuts, rice, and plantains.

There were horses, cows, and many other animals out in the open. It was there that, thanks to God, life was so happy. We used to gather coconuts, carrying them down from the trees. I was tall, and the school was very far away, but with effort and faith, I managed to return.

There were times and attempts, but those days came to an end. When I wanted to stay, I had to leave because of circumstances. I suffered, but God never abandoned me. I remember being happy when my father took care of us.

My brothers and I grew up beautifully, free in the countryside, happy in God's air. We ate what my father gave us, by the blessing of God and by my father's wife. I owed everything to him. We were never poor in spirit, and we were not troubled. Our home had everything we needed.

My father cared for us and worked. I was only thirty-five years old, surviving my life, already accustomed to it. I felt powerless, unable to do anything. My daughter was already grown and married. I was preparing to move to Puerto Plata with great faith, trusting that God would guide me. He never abandoned me.

Reflecting on everything, the trials, the struggles, I realized I had my daughter, but I could not always be there for her. Now she is an adult, and I did not fall behind. Little by little, everything began to calm me, filling me with peace and the courage to press forward.

I believe that God watches over us, never allowing us to face more than we can bear. I feel it was a miracle; my time to live and to write my story. Humility, health, and family: these are the blessings I cherish the most. I rose in the world because of my mother. Thanks be to God that I was able to overcome all this time. The days of the past are gone.

Chapter V

Faith, Gratitude, and Family

The Strength of God in My Life

*"I am a woman who was once very strong, very sad,
and also very happy."*

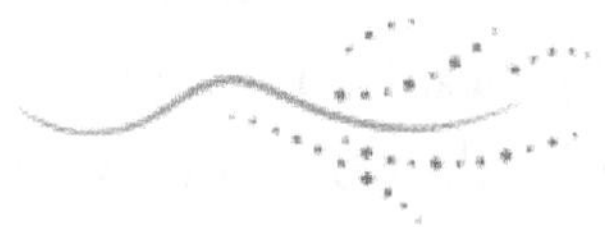

When I had my children, I had to say goodbye to my former self. Every step I took was by grace, moving forward with the strength of God. My grandmother and my mother are no longer here; they have passed on. But those who believe know that I fulfilled my purpose and gave thanks to God.

I went through difficult stages, but those hardships taught me real lessons in life. With strength, I continued, and now I am passing through a time of peace. When my children grew, everything changed; I was no longer the same as before. As a child, I remember how happy my life was when I played as a girl.

My mother used to tell me stories about her grandmother. I often laughed at my own little things. My mother cared for me deeply. Now, God, I am at peace; I no longer long for sadness. It was my mother's love and God's care that made everything possible.

My son and I are no longer who we were, but through the strength of God, we press on. Thanks be to God, He has kept me in the faith. He never let me go. He sat with me through everything. I am a woman who was once very strong, very sad, but also very happy.

Now I am working, as I said before. Today I live with peace and tranquility. I did not grow up in the countryside, but I have been formed through faith and inner peace. I always share the lessons that life has taught me.

I remember the years spent with my grandmother; I remember the moments we shared. As children, we played and worked hard. I continue to breathe life into each new day. I am grateful because I was given the opportunity, the faith, and the possibility to live. Before, I could not, but now I can.

Today, I have strength through work, food, memory, and faith. I do not forget my past, but I move forward with determination. From this moment on, I am grateful, for myself and for my parents, because I found satisfaction in life.

I make a petition to God, to the Virgin, to my mother, and to my children. The Virgin of Altagracia is everything to me, and after her, my son always remains in my heart. I am grateful. Nothing takes away my faith. The Virgin of Altagracia keeps me faithful; she is the one who grants me peace, powerful and strong. I never want to lose that.

After everything, I trust in work and in joy. My husband is no longer the same, but my grandparents were so affectionate. My grandmothers, over the years, showed me love and kindness. That love changes over time, especially when one finally has everything one needs.

Today I walk with my son, who gives me strength. I no longer feel sadness, only fullness. Thanks be to God, to my faith, to my children, and to my family. They bring me peace and deepen my faith. God has kept me steadfast; I cannot deny it.

I believe in everything God has given me. By the grace of God, I trust that He believes in everything I am. I only ask to always be happy. I ask for nothing more than to keep going forward, always as I am, with faith, strength, and work. That is enough.

With strength, family, and love, wherever I go, wherever I wish to be, I pray to always be near Him. Stay with me forever. Thank you, always, for the faith, the spirit, the affection, and the respect.

I was ill with many things; I had pain in my heart. When they gave me the little bottle, things happened. Thanks to God and to medicine, I was able to find help. It was very sad that that little bottle they gave me… without it, perhaps I would have given up. It brought me peace, though I was very tired. With the passage of time, I returned to my path.

When I met her, it was my grandmother, always present in those memories of mine. Even as a very small girl, I felt her presence. She would leave, but I would no longer die. I remembered her love. Why? Because of my mother.

Thank you, because she stayed with me, and it was the same with my father; my mother was always fighting for life to continue, for the struggle to go on. In my difficult days, I thank God that I found support. I find people along my path who follow me and keep me moving.

I have something ahead of me: a purpose. I am never alone. An angel came to me and said, "Faith, faith." A woman who reminds me of my grandmother, the Virgin of Altagracia. "Thank you," she says to me.

Through her words, I know it is not always easy. My grandmother tells me, "No more suffering, no more, for your children's sake." I do not want to suffer anymore. I think of when I used to play, when my mother gave me love. Those memories stay with me, and I hold fast to faith, hope, and gratitude.

My strength comes from health, tradition, and faith; faith for living. When I give thanks, I remember my beginnings. It was on July 20, 1993, that my faith began to grow. That was the beginning of my journey. I ask myself: why judge me? It is not right to judge.

Only in a health class might someone question the body, but faith remains my foundation. I continue to be happy, especially in my marriage, but more than that, I continue to be happy because of my faith. Thank you, God, for my son, for my children, and for my life; so strong and full of purpose.

With the strength of God, I value my family and the necessities such as food and clothing. I did not always recognize these blessings before, but now I do. Thank you, God, for life. I remember everything I have thanks to Your strength. I never forget my family, my children, or my loved ones.

With peace, with health, and with God, for all of this, I am happy. No more worries, only gratitude.

Chapter VI

The Flavors of My Life

The Land That Shaped Me

*"The guayo and the pineapple, that fruit taught
me to live."*

I t is like my land and my father; may God grant him health and well-being. I pray for my little ones, my children, Celeddy and Álvaro; they are so happy. All that is missing is my mother for everything to be complete. I love my family, even though I have not yet learned everything, but I believe every Christian must be saintly, guided by divine strength.

My mother was not with me, but I had faith. The light never abandoned me; my sister Sonia helped with her upbringing. I give thanks to God because, through them, I am leaving behind the hardships of my youth.

For everything that exists in this land, I carry you in my heart. I learned from you, and I give thanks to God for my family and for my son. I give thanks to God for myself, for being a strong and traditional person. I feel very powerful in my happiness. I thank God even for the solitude, for the peace I have now.

I remember my fifteenth year, something I never truly lived at that age. Now, looking at myself at this age, I cannot believe it. The grater and the pineapple, that fruit taught me to live. I remember those small things: selling charcoal on a little donkey and gathering firewood. Who would have thought those moments were truly mine? Even eating beside the firewood as a girl, thanks be to God.

My God, thank you for giving me solutions, for life, for health, and for a wonderful family. Thank you for my children. Thank you for giving me faith. Do not think that sin does not exist; God is no less for it. We must not judge anyone.

Through hard work, we do not sleep in laziness, we do not lie, and we do not give up. Always be humble, read well, and learn much; faith will guide you. Not everything is about fame, but with education, one can go far. Keep persevering and triumphing; that is life.

Once I was a poor girl, but that no longer matters to me. I remember the difficult months, eating pumpkin (auyama) with allspice and rice with coconut—delicious food. All that matters now is how happy I am.

I love my father because he was there, but being a mother is different; it is filled with a unique affection. Now I always need that love. The vows I once believed in sometimes make me feel unwell when I come to know the truth. I know it always feels like family, even when one is sometimes rejected by those less fortunate or by poverty.

Such is life: sometimes full of pain and rejection, but we press on. In spite of being poor and renouncing many things of the world, I know that one day I will arrive. That thought was difficult at first, but through faith I found strength; faith in a better future, in hope, and in God's plan for me. Even in the difficult moments, I hold onto life's beautiful game, trusting that everything will come together.

I will never forget where I come from. I am proud of my country, and I give thanks to God for it. My childhood was hard, but my maternal grandparents allowed me to dream. My parents were very hardworking and loved everything they did. The beautiful sight of a banana grove, one of the most beautiful views, is like a pumpkin with leaves. Dried plantains, grapes, cloth, old rice, belladonna, and the dry banana leaf: these were the flavors of my life. Thank you, my God.

Plantains and laughter; that is how we shared our meals with faith. Like the rice with milk from the old country ranch, my faith was always in the group, in God, and in the Virgin of Altagracia, the divine presence that has always been with us. Among the things I treasure, the plantain stands out as a symbol of life's simple joys. My brother and I never complained; we were always grateful. I helped my parents with the "guayacos" of things, and I planted what I could.

No one was different. To the outside world, we were all the same: the guayaceros, the ones who planted, the small ones. In my humble reality, I say to my siblings: a mother's love is forever. She was the best woman in the world.

We endured so much, especially in times of scarcity, and they treated us differently, because some were my father's children, born into poverty. My mother was with my father, and I always thought of his children. For the great values you taught me, I love you, Father. Thank you for the memories. I believe God has him in a good place, happy, even though he did not know the same pain that I feel in my body.

I deny that my mother was weak, but when she spoke to me frankly, I saw her pain. She would look at the sky and feel sorrow. From that little house below, I do not despair. Alone and lonely, I feel like a little girl again, clinging to my grandmother's things, my only star. It hurts, but it is the sweetest thing in the world.

I would lie in her lap and fall asleep as she told me stories. She would gently comb my little eyebrows; she was the best. I love you, Grandmother. How I adore you. She used to tell me, "We did well." She reminded me of the importance of learning from her and from my grandmother, Rafael's stories. Those were always wonderful times.

I worked hard to become something. Before, I had a language, a language of respect. Back then, everyone in the world was dear to one another; we always carried that in our hearts. I remember playing with my siblings: horses, hair, donkeys, and "al hoyito." I remember having a scar on my leg where a horse kicked me; it hardened with time. There were washboards and my father straining at his work; yet more bitter than that was the taste of lemon. What times those were. What a country, so beautiful, always. You were, and you remain, great and protective.

But something happens, and life changes. A doctor used to tell me, "The sun will shine again." We keep walking through the passage of time. I always excelled at mathematics because reading was my gift, and so was writing. Those were my strengths. I reached far and kept going. At a certain point, I thought I had died and, somehow, the conclusion of living arrived. We had to leave our studies because we had nothing. Yet, in spite of everything, those memories remain with me: strong and enduring.

We did not speak much of "things." We moved from one town to another, through the middle of a guava grove, without a key. Poverty was always on the same road, always the same, accompanied by humility. I guided the little ducklings; since we did not know much of luxurious clothing, its absence did not pain us. Only the shoes mattered, and sometimes we could not even find those. The difference was clear. That is why some families never saw our struggle; we were always the small ones. We recognized the value of small things, like plates. I remember presenting them with joy.

After leaving, I moved to a place near the coconuts. My work, my contribution; working the roads—was serious work that required serious effort. When my children came, even though we had no house or material things (which are not important), my brother and I always sowed the right path, giving our best. I worked from a very young age, but always with humility, aiming high. My experience with my father guided me, and I carried with great pride the honor of being his daughter, a different kind of faith.

Grandmother had a beautiful cousin: tall, ten years old, the same age as my mother. She taught me to be still, like a small girl, innocent at that age, to speak in silence. She herself did not speak much; she only worked and worked.

Epilogue

There are books written so the world may know; this book was written so that I myself might see me. In the act of ordering memories, I discovered that my life, in spite of all the pain, holds a beautiful architecture: every trial was the foundation of a fortress that cannot be seen from outside, but is felt deeply within.

When I think of the girl who ran barefoot through the fields, who rode horses before dawn, who gave birth under conditions that would have broken anyone, and who prayed fervently in borrowed churches, I feel a pride that cannot be contained in words.

That girl is me. And this woman who now writes these lines, with the peace of the countryside and the faith of always—she is also me.

The color of rebirth is not just one. It is the green of the grass I cut at dawn, the white of the horse that carried me far, the red of the earth that watched me grow, and the gold of the faith that never, never abandoned me.

Acknowledgments

To my mother Paula, who was my backbone and my first home: everything I am began in your arms.

To my children Celeddy and Álvaro, who are the most tangible proof that miracles are not merely stories: living them was the greatest gift of my life.

To my sister Sonia, who carried what I could not carry and loved my children as if they were her own.

To Mrs. Rosa, may God hold her in His glory: her kindness reminded me that the world holds good people even in its darkest moments.

To the Virgin of Altagracia, constant presence, silent strength, refuge always open.

And to all those who shared a plate of food, a word of encouragement, or an outstretched hand along the way: this book belongs to you as well.

About the Author

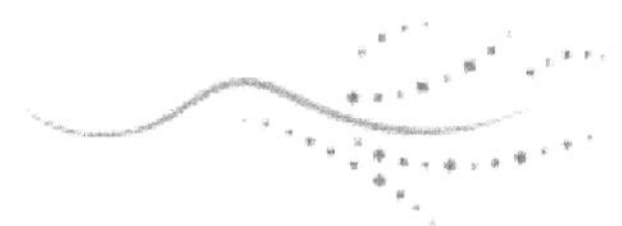

B orn on July 7, 1980, in the Dominican countryside, Luci Partela, author of The Color of Rebirth, grew up among goats, coconut palms, banana trees, and the unshakeable faith of a humble family. From childhood, she learned that work, the land, and devotion are not burdens, but the very materials from which a dignified life is built.

Throughout her life, she faced losses, displacement, illness, and childbirth under extraordinary conditions, finding in each instance the same resource: faith. A mother, a tireless worker, and a guardian of family memory, she chose to write her story not to complain about what she suffered, but to give thanks for what she survived.

This is her first book. She dedicates it to her children, to her mother, and to all those who once walked down muddy roads with wet shoes—and arrived, nonetheless, at exactly where they needed to be.